Promptings

Kimberly Malkogainnis

Promptings

© 2012 by Kimberly Malkogainnis

Published by Next Step Books, P.O. Box 70271, West Valley City, Utah 84170

Cover design by Next Step Books, LLC.

Malkogainnis, Kimberly

Promptings

ISBN-13: 978-1-937671-10-5

ISBN-10: 1937671100

About *Promptings*

In *Promptings*, Kimberly Malkogainnis opens her heart and invites us into the deepest recesses of her soul with beautiful prose and powerful poetry. I found myself in these pages.

> ~ Virginia Smith
> Bestselling Author of *Bullseye*
> and *The Heart's Frontier*

Kimberly Malkogainnis captivates the reader with honesty and wisdom gained through experiences with which most people can identify, either personally or through the challenges of family or friends. I was going to read a few pages at a time but when I began, I couldn't put it down until I read the last word.

> ~ Amy Barkman
> Author of *Murder at Tapestry Court*
> and *Everyday Spiritual Warfare*

Kimberly has a gift for words and a ministry of encouragement. Her creative prose, provocative poetry, and *aha* endings will delight and inspire you to draw close to God. Despite unwanted circumstances and negative emotions you may have, let Kimberly prompt you to trust your Father's loyal love.

> ~ Marcia Hornok, Managing Editor
> *CHERA Fellowship* magazine for widowed persons

Kimberly Malkogainnis journeys through life experiences ranging from the painful to the delightful to learn God's lessons. As I read *Promptings*, I was drawn closer to God.

Kimberly Malkogainnis kidnapped my heart from the very first paragraph in *Promptings* until the last line. Time and again her undisguised honesty resonated in my soul.

In *Promptings* Kim Malkogainnis shares her own spiritual journey in short, compelling snapshots. Every time I set it down, I picked it up again to read another page or two—until suddenly the book was finished and I wanted more.

Promptings is dedicated to my Lord and
Savior Jesus Christ,
To Whom I owe my eternal salvation...

Special thanks to:
Andrew Malkogainnis, the husband who
supports and encourages my writing ministry;
Grandma Vivian, who gave me my first Bible
and my first typewriter;
and the members of Utah Christian Writers
Fellowship,
who helped so much with the publication of
this book.

Contents

Thomas and the Doubter

I pulled the blue curtain aside and gazed flatly out the window at the road in front of my house. The large naked willow in my yard endorsed my mood with its weeping limbs.

As it does so frequently in our area, a winter inversion had formed a lid that sealed in the poisonous color of industrial waste and vehicle exhaust. I glumly noted the thick brown smog which had settled in the valley.

How appropriate, I thought, a *day nearly as bleak as my life...*

There was no sign of my husband, Andrew, who had left the house several hours earlier to tend to some paperwork associated with his three-month-old back injury. I let go of the curtains and sighed heavily before flopping down on the sofa in a disgusted heap.

For years, Andrew had been the sole supporter of our household. We had grown accustomed to the security of a regular paycheck; but then Andrew took a fateful tumble down his employer's unlighted staircase. Suddenly, God's provider was disabled with back pain, unable to work. The normalcy of daily life was replaced by frequent visits to a doctor with a worried looking face and a dismal diagnosis.

I shuddered at the possibility that my husband's pain might never end, and I fearfully wondered how we would make ends meet when the meager workman's compensation payments were exhausted. Would we join the growing ranks of homeless families?

The uncertainty of the situation, coupled with my own chronic health problems, weighed heavily on me. My life seemed to be one big question mark. A sense of helplessness overwhelmed me.

Oh God... I moaned, *I'm so afraid. I don't know what to do—where to turn. If Andrew can't work, how will we get by?*

The heavens appeared to be silent on the subject. I let my head fall into my hands as tears of doubt and apprehension rolled down my cheeks.

The banging of a car door in the driveway roused me from my thoughts. Assuming it must be Andrew returning home, I hurriedly dried my eyes and wiped my face. He had enough on his mind already, and I didn't want him to know I'd been crying. I didn't know that God had begun to prepare an answer to my prayer even before it was uttered.

I went to the front door and opened it. As I stepped out onto the lattice-covered porch, I was greeted by the surprisingly cheerful face of my husband. I wondered what he had to smile about. After all, our world was crashing down upon us.

Andrew's arms were twisted awkwardly to one side, both hands covering one of the large pockets in his red ski vest. Curiosity momentarily chased my gloom and I moved toward him for closer inspection.

"What are you hiding?" I playfully demanded.

In response to my inquiry, Andrew slowly and gently extracted the contents of the pocket. In one hand, he held out a tiny, grey tabby kitten.

"O-h-h-h," I murmured, instinctively reaching for the infant feline. He mewed frantically as Andrew transferred him to my outstretched hands. I carefully hugged the kitten to me and he snuggled under my chin.

"I found him on the road," explained Andrew, softly stroking the kitten's shivering body. "I almost didn't see the little guy. He blended in with the grey pavement."

"On the *road*?!" I asked incredulously.

"Poor baby," I said, examining the frail head. "Look. His nose is all scuffed up."

I carried the kitten into the warmth of the house. Andrew followed us inside, and continued his tale of rescue.

"There was no mother cat or any litter mates around. He was all alone, dodging traffic."

Andrew sat uncomfortably on the couch, his face betraying the pain that accompanied even simple movements.

"He doesn't have much in the way of teeth," I commented. "I bet he isn't even weaned yet."

"I know we don't need another mouth to feed—especially with our lives in such a mess—" he began.

"It's okay," I interrupted him. "You couldn't leave him alone and in danger. I would've brought him home, too." I thought about how confused and frightened the kitten must have been before Andrew scooped him up. "God must have sent you with your soft heart to save him. He knows and cares when a sparrow falls from its nest. I guess that goes for kittens, too."

As the familiar passage of scripture echoed in my mind, the conviction of God gripped my doubting heart. "But even the very hairs of your head are numbered. Fear not, therefore; ye are of more value than many sparrows." (Luke 12:7, NIV)

Fear not. I knew the command. *Ye are of more value than many sparrows.* I was aware of the provision. I believed it applied to little tomcats, but I had forgotten my own value in the eyes of my Lord and Savior.

I looked down again at the kitten pressed tightly against me and listened momentarily to his faint purring punctuated by anxious bouts of mewing. How alike we were—both of us scared and crying for security that was ours already, oblivious to the capable arms that surrounded us with loving protection. As I contemplated the sufficiency of the God I worshipped, I felt ashamed at my distrust of Him. Silently, I confessed my faithlessness. The unexpected answer to my earlier plea for reassurance continued to squirm in my arms.

The kitten who came to us a survivor of life-threatening adversity eventually acquired the name, "Thomas." He grew into a handsome cat with mischievous green eyes and freckles that dotted the protrusion of each whisker around his eraser-colored nose. He was a faithful companion throughout prolonged and frustrating negotiations over Andrew's injury.

The doctor had initially given my husband a limited release for employment with the stipulation that he not lift over 25 pounds. But because of our financial situation and lack of health insurance, Andrew was unable to have any form of therapy or treatment.

He continued to receive workman's compensation for a few months longer. However, when the carrier learned that Andrew's disability might be permanent, he was required to see their designated physician. Not surprisingly, the company determined that the fall down the stairs was not the cause of his back pain. Thus, the claim was denied and he was refused further benefits. Then his employer terminated him.

Andrew was unable to find permanent full-time work for four years, but in incredible ways, God provided for our needs—even giving us enough to share with others. The occurrences of these "little miracles" were always divinely timed to stretch our faith.

There was the time Andrew stopped to help a stranded woman change a flat tire on the freeway and she insisted on giving him $20 for his services...and the anonymous $300 gift that came in the mail one particularly needy day. There was the Christian friend who was moving out of state who gave us everything in her pantry and freezer. The extra duties for which Andrew volunteered with the National Guard helped him train for a career that would not strain his back. He maintains that job to this day.

I believe it is my fallen, human nature to have doubts. Thomas' entrance into our lives certainly did not put an end to all anxiety or challenges. But I know now that I can choose to cast my cares on God rather than immersing myself in destructive fear.

Until I wept as he lay dying in my arms eight years ago at the age of twenty, Thomas remained a daily visual reminder that God's agenda is not necessarily the same as ours.

The Lord is willing to be faithful in every circumstance. I may not like His methods. I may not always understand them. But the choice to doubt—or trust—is mine.

Wedding Prayer

The many-colored patches in this quilt are like the different facets of your two personalities. Each hue retains its own unique qualities as it comes together in harmony with the others to create a thing of beauty.

The inner layer of batting supplies the warmth and softness, just as your mutual respect will be a buffer against a sometimes cold, harsh world.

The threads pull together opposite sides. I pray that the joy and pain, trials and triumphs you will encounter in the years ahead will draw each of you to the other in a deepening commitment.

The binding surrounds and fastens the quilt, covering its raw edges. May the love you proclaim this day serve to cover one another's faults and idiosyncrasies with patient acceptance.

As I lovingly joined together the patches, ties, batting and binding one piece at a time, I kept in mind the value and pleasure that the finished product would provide. May you keep the same optimistic vision about your marriage.

This wedding quilt is my gift to you both as the two become one.

The Storm

A storm sweeps through my life,
     leaving rubble and
wreckage
       in its wake.
So I attempt to
fan a spark of gratitude
      with positive thinking
      and a pious version of
Pollyanna's
     glad game.
But preconceived notions
     and arrogance and pain
dampen my zeal.
         I am unable.
Suddenly my soul is afire with
that which I
could not muster with human
effort,

11

and I perceive that thankfulness,
like all else I offer You, is
simply returning that
which
You have first imparted to me.

Flowers for my Birthday

I was spending my birthday alone. And I wasn't happy about it.

So I decided to throw myself a pity party. I donned a cloak of gloom and serenaded myself with a lamentation: *Poor me. I'm getting old. Poor me. I'm getting wrinkled.* I sniveled and mentally moaned for most of the morning.

I was still ankle-deep in misery when a florist's truck stopped in front of my house. Through the window, I saw a man carrying a glorious bunch of flowers. *Who,* I wondered gleefully, *had sent this wonderful birthday bouquet?* I hurried to meet the driver at the front gate.

"Would you be willing to accept delivery of these flowers?" he asked. "The person I'm supposed to deliver to isn't home."

I said it was okay with me, hoping that saying it would make it true. Trying to squelch my disappointment, I took someone else's flowers into my house and set them on the counter. *No fair*, I whined. *It's my birthday.*

Late afternoon arrived, but the flowers' rightful recipient had not. Determined to be rid of the mocking blooms, I carried the fragrant spray to the correct address.

"These were delivered to my house today," I told the man I met there. "They're for Leslie. Is that you?" Without waiting for an answer, I thrust the flowers at him.

"Leslie's my wife," he said, choking on his words. "We've had a death in the family."

He looked at me with red-rimmed eyes, holding the flowers I had coveted. A wave of guilt washed over me, and the undertow left me momentarily weak.

"I'm sorry," was all I could muster as I turned to leave.

I went home, fell on my middle-aged knees and cried out to God with a child's heart. *Oh, Lord*, I prayed, *how could I have been so selfish and spoiled? I've spent the day whining because no one was celebrating my birthday. Yet my neighbor is weeping over a loved one whose birthday will never come again. I wanted to be pampered when I should have been finding ways to serve. I thought I deserved gifts to unwrap; I know now all I really need is to stop being wrapped up in myself.*

I penned a note of sympathy to my grieving neighbor, all the while praising God for blessings I'd earlier discounted: sunshine and laugh-lines and memories, and the eternal life that is mine because I accepted Christ as my Savior on a special re-birth day years earlier.

The aroma of that bouquet has long since faded, but its lesson was an enduring one. And so I find myself on subsequent birthdays thanking the Lord for those beautiful flowers. Flowers never really intended for me.

Or were they?

Like Father

Someone I love is bent beneath the
weight
                of a wounded spirit.
The cruelty inflicted was deliberate,
            and I am angry at the one
                    who committed the wrong.

Yet, He was your innocent One,
            Your Son, who was mocked
                    and scourged,
            spit on,
            and slain...

Like mine, Your heart was broken;
            like me You felt a kinsman's
pain.
And so, like You,
            I must heap loving kindness

upon those who are brutal,
ever mindful that mercy is the
sinner's *only* hope,
praying for strength to forgive
that which is impossible to forget.

Expectations

Abs of steel, compact buns,
        low body fat, high income;
freshest breath, full head of hair,
        a mate must have and then
some.

Virtue's a low priority,
        commitment is disparaged,
and we wonder why it's thriving,
        divorce, I mean, not
marriage.

Dragon Mommy

Ellen and her son, Matthew, stood in the hallway, just beyond earshot of his first grade classmates. Ellen's eyes glowed a bloody red as she vented her anger. The venomous words shot out, accompanied by hot, billowing smoke.

"Maybe if I let you go hungry today, you won't forget your lunch again!" she snapped, glaring down at Matthew's six-year-old face.

"But I—I get so hungry at lunchtime..." he said softly. Brown eyes, full of tears, revealed the fear and confusion he felt. He wondered what force had transformed this one he knew as a loving mother into the merciless creature that hovered over him.

"You know," reminded Ellen, barbed tail thumping, "this is the *third* time you've forgotten your lunch!"

Ellen ignored the taste of brimstone in her mouth.

"I know—I'm sorry..." said Matthew, and looked down at the floor. A tear dropped from his cheek and made a wet spot on the toe of his sneaker.

"Sometimes you are so irresponsible!" Ellen continued.

Digging her talons into the carpet, she paused to consider the time required to retrieve the forgotten meal. The time would have to be extracted from a full, hectic schedule since the private school had no lunch program. She was angry, and her son's apparent remorse was insufficient to soothe the beast in her.

Ellen lifted Matthew's chin with an unsheathed claw and peered into his face. "I'm going to go home and get your lunch," she relented, glowering, "but if this ever happens again, you *will* go hungry!"

She said good-bye and left him standing outside the classroom, his baby-fine hair still smoking from the fiery reprimand.

As Ellen drove home, she squirmed uncomfortably in her seat. She began to recall times innumerable she had displeased God by repeated disobedience. The Lord's reaction to her behavior had been forgiveness and guidance. Even at that moment, His hand remained outstretched.

Does my son deserve less from me for a simple act of forgetfulness? She asked herself and God at the same time.

As she clumsily maneuvered the car into the driveway of her home, Ellen mentally noted that modern vehicles were not designed with dragon mommies in mind.

And neither, she thought, heaving a sigh that filled the interior with a sulfuric-smelling mist, *were little boys.*

She leaned her head on the steering wheel, bumping the crooked horn that protruded from between her eyes. *O Lord*, she prayed, *forgive me for frustrating and inflicting emotional abuse on the little one You have entrusted to me.* She determined to ask her son's forgiveness upon returning to school.

As Ellen confessed her selfishness and impatience, she felt the menacing fangs disappear. The sharp claws retracted when she resolved to rethink a schedule that left her cranky and rushed.

Perhaps, she thought, *I will take two lunches—one for Matthew and one for myself.* Ellen contemplated the specialness of a "date" with her son, and her scaly exterior softened.

Tears born of repentance washed the fire from Ellen's eyes. And she stepped out of the car on two feet of clay.

Words

Chink. Nigger. Bum.

Fatso. Stupid. Retard.

Words

That become labels

And conjure derogatory mental
images—

That perpetuate hatred.

Savior. Grace. Mercy.

Charity. Agape. Prayer.

Words

That possess power

To break down fleshly facades

That obscure souls for whom He
died.

Kimberly Malkogainnis

Holiday Religion

I primp in festive attire, and give
trinkets that now
    evoke a smile but later gather
dust behind
    closed doors.
Others long for a secure place to rest
tired bodies,
    and a covering for bare, cold
limbs.
I thrill to colored lights. Others shiver
in the moonlight.
I feast and complain that my diet is
spoiled.
    Others feel stomachs rumble a
reminder
    of meals missed.
I take for granted the nearness of those
I love.

    Others ache for a compassionate
touch—
    an understanding smile.
The widow is uncomforted. The
fatherless knows
    no love.
On this spiritual holiday, my religion is
impure.

Bendable Agenda

The Gospels tell us plainly that Jesus Christ spent His earthly life attending to His Father's business. He expelled demons, instructed His followers, forgave sin, healed the sick and debated with local religious leaders. At the end of His thirty-three years, Jesus endured a criminal's death on the cross. He defeated sin and Satan when He burst from the grave in glory.

With all of this done, there was still much more for Jesus to accomplish. The Almighty awaited His return to Heaven, and His scattered, confused followers desperately needed the training, unification and power of the Spirit that Jesus would soon impart.

In the midst of this bustle, the apostle John inserted in his Gospel a picture of Mary.

She stood outside the open tomb, weeping bitterly. Her heart was broken by the recent tragedy of Jesus' death. Her faith and hope had been extinguished, and her despairing thoughts would not allow her hopes to be lifted—even by the presence of Heavenly angels at the tomb.

There was a time in my life when I likely would have rushed past this broken one, all puffed up and muttering about all the things I needed to get done. Yet even with His divinely appointed docket, Christ did not ignore Mary.

There were times when fervor to complete my self-imposed schedule caused me to divert my attention from eyes filled with apprehension or pain or longing. I rationalized that I must check projects off my "to do" list as I impatiently opened my brimming day planner instead of my empty heart.

But the Lord paused in His wondrous agenda to speak a name in love. He cared enough to soothe the tattered emotions of one weary, distressed follower.

Christ's actions convey much about the importance He places on the individual.

Showing tenderness to a grieving woman was part of His plan, not an interruption of it.

It has been said that time is the dressing room for eternity. When the curtain goes up and I step onto the stage of the Hereafter, I do not believe God will extol my ability to meet a deadline, sit on a committee, or finish my busy work.

I think He will, instead, ask for a show of hands—the ones I paused long enough to hold.

Before Your Throne

Before Your throne,
I bring the agony of a broken
heart.
I heap on You the anxiety that
comes from living in a
fallen world.
To You, I confess my pride,
my greed,
my vanity.
At Your feet, I question,
worship,
grieve,
rejoice.
I share with You my anger, and
my love.
Lord of Lords, Alpha and Omega,
The one thing I cannot
bring before Your throne
is a surprise.

Kimberly Malkogainnis

Bill of Rights

Lord,
   From the darkness
      I proclaimed my right
  to feel comfort,
  to exact vengeance,
  to glorify self,
  to celebrate pride.
I sought self-control
and ultimate rule.

But Your light has illumined the Truth.
   It is You, O Lord,
     not I,
Who is
   center of the universe.

Your love created all things;
   Your mercy binds them together.

You Knew It

Today, my world splintered and crashed...
> My tormented heart begged to know
why.

> Yet, You were not stunned
> > by my outcry.

Before You made the worlds by Your Word,
before You came
> to pour out Your blood
> and love on Calvary,
before I breathed a single breath,
> You knew that today
> > I would shake my fist at the
> Heavens...

and You lovingly caressed that fist,
> mingled Your tears with mine,

31

and assured me that however deep the pain—

You knew it.

Your Voice

My dead spirit writhed in the agony of its
sinfulness.
I was lost,
doomed to eternal Hell.
Then I read the Word
that irresistibly drew me.

> *I am the door...enter in by Me...*
> *And be saved...*

I cowered and dreaded the morning.
Then the voice of Your thunder shook my
fear.
Lightning illumined my doubt.
In Your creation, I heard the Word that
comforted me.

> *Don't let your heart be troubled...*
> *Trust me...*

I was sorrowful, bent beneath the weight of
my pain.

Then the voice of Your servant echoed the
Word
that strengthened me.

>   *Come to me and I will give you rest...*

Sin,
fear,
and pain
are powerless against the Word
that lets me hear Your voice from Heaven.

Sunday Morning

"Good morning, Jane," said Mrs. Brock,
"And how are you today?"
"I'm feeling fine," was Jane's reply,
"You look elegant in grey!"

They chatted at length about their clothes,
and the warm spell that had hit.
But neither let her guard down—
neither would take the risk.

Jane didn't mention her agony
o'er a marriage that was broken.
Of Mrs. Brock's struggle with sin,
not one word was spoken.

So each woman left the service
with an aching, troubled heart,
each bearing her own burdens,

and not the other's part.

Both of the women suffered alone.
And no one offered a prayer.
No comfort could be given—
because nobody dared to share.

New Heart's
Resolutions

Father, in the coming days
    I want to spend less time
    looking down on my brother,
    more time on my knees
  interceding for him.
    I want to be adept
        at holding my sister's hand,
        not in shaking a finger at her.
Let me shoulder others' burdens
    instead of casting stones.
Give me a spirit willing
    to forgo its rights
In favor of what is upright.
    Lord, transform these resolutions
  into realities.

Living with Killing

The clinic counselor was supportive. Reveling in the sympathy she offered, I failed to realize her job description probably included showing kindness to potential money-paying clients. She listened quietly to my tale of accidental conception, desertion and distorted emotions. Then the woman pushed some papers across the desk.

"You'll need to read this information and then sign here," she pointed to a blank line on the form, "to signify you understand everything you've read, and agree to the procedure."

Procedure. A carefully selected euphemism designed to dull the human conscience to the heinous realities of abortion. I signed the contract without reading it.

In the beginning, though unmarried and unsaved, I wanted to keep and nurture the child within me. I sewed maternity clothes, designed a baby quilt and looked forward to holding my newborn in my arms. Then my life became a blur of anger, loud advice and pointing fingers.

The desire to end the emotional torment demanded that I squelch the God-instilled maternal instinct. I reluctantly made an appointment with a local women's clinic and pretended my decision was the sensible one.

With the paperwork completed, I was escorted to a cool, antiseptic room and told to disrobe. The assistant provided me with a disposable paper gown to put on and left the room. It seemed that a lot of things there were disposable. She returned a few moments later, accompanied by the physician who would slay my child.

The doctor was abrupt and impatient as he stretched on his rubber gloves. Perhaps, like me, he was hurrying in order to evade a pursuing conscience.

"Okay," instructed the man who switched on a high-intensity lamp near my feet, "just lie back and relax."

The room was filled with the loud hum of a murderous machine. I concentrated hard on the abstract pattern of dots on the ceiling as tears rolled onto the small pillow beneath my head. The anesthesia I'd been given hadn't worked, and my abdomen began to burn with unquenchable pain. I writhed in agony as my baby's miniature, but fully-formed limbs and childish face were suctioned away in bloody fragments.

Anguish of body and soul swallowed me. I silently told my child good-bye just before I lost consciousness.

"Kimberly!" The assistant's voice intruded into my place of quiet blackness. "Kimberly!" she repeated more urgently.

I squinted up at the harsh fluorescent lights to see the shape of her form hovering over me.

"It's over," she announced more calmly, "you blacked out on us. You were having an unusual amount of pain."

Pain is fitting, I told myself, *someone was dying.*

As I limply sat in the recovery area, I sipped 7-up and studied the faces of the other women there. Our ages varied. Our dress and backgrounds were different.

Yet we shared an awful bond—and a common expression. Each of us had endorsed the killing of a child. Strained smiles and sad eyes disclosed the state of our hearts.

The security and safety of the womb had been invaded by the surgeon's blade. Our mangled children now filled sanitary containers destined for the pathology lab. There they would be examined to determine if they were, indeed, the *product of conception.* Another euphemism.

No funerals. No grieving. Just simple disposal of unwanted waste.

My post-abortion recovery was different from what I'd been promised. It wasn't quick or painless. There were complications, both physical and mental.

Like raising a child, dealing with the aftermath of the abortion became a full-time commitment. There were no joys or trials of parenthood, no childish smile, no heart-warming, "I love you, Mommy." There was only pain in varying degrees, and longing with each thought or mention of the word *abortion.*

My mind couldn't endure reality's torture. I determined to deal with the facts at some later date, and buried guilt and grief beneath excuses and misdirected blame.

Years later, I appropriated Christ's sacrificial death on my behalf and committed myself to Him. I possessed new life, but the memory of my child's murder haunted me still. I saw the abortion as a sin too ghastly to be forgiven. I became my own pitiless judge.

However, God's love was too complete to allow me to continue executing a sentence of cruel mental torture. On a still evening, alone with Him, he began to expose my emotional wound to the purifying light of His love.

He had removed my sin "as far as the east is from the west" (Psalm 103:12 NIV) when I first trusted Him to save me. Now He wanted me to pardon *myself.*

Earlier in the day I had selected several tracts from an attractive rack in the Christian book store I frequented. One of the pamphlets detailed the physical and spiritual realities of abortion.

As the facts sunk into my brain, an emotional war raged within me. Part of me wanted to put down the tract—to continue the cycle of self-torment. But the Holy Spirit in me was unrelenting in His demand for purging.

Worn from years of reliving my child's death, the sorrow began to pour forth in torrents of tears that I could not control. Surely then the Spirit interceded, for my pain formed few words. Years of remorse oozed like infection from the wound.

I felt myself being emptied of bitterness and guilt. The mental bandaging began to fall away. I was, at last, able to mourn my dear baby. Into the resulting void, God infused a completing peace that the Almighty can share only with one of His own.

I relinquished my sin to a more merciful Judge, and laid the killing at the foot of the cross where the Savior's blood covered the blood of my slain child. I felt a suffocating heaviness lift from my soul, and sat for a long time, basking in the warmth of forgiveness I'd long denied myself.

Just as He did centuries before, my God equipped the lame to walk. He infused strength into crippled emotions. His loving touch brought clear vision where once self-recrimination had blinded.

I cannot forget the person I once was—or the crime perpetrated on the most helpless of victims. But I have forsaken my sin. I have finally forgiven myself because I have felt the healing touch of the Savior's nail-scarred hand.

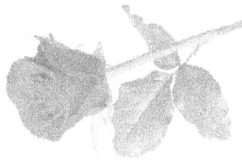

Divine Docket

Luck and chance are Satan's lies.
Each moment of this new day
is divinely docketed.

And although I am incapable
of fully comprehending Your design,
I can most assuredly trust it.

Kimberly Malkogainnis

The Comforter

Fraught with frustration, I sat on the edge of my bed, sobbing myself soggy. I was so miserable that I didn't even want to "talk it out" with someone.

Reclining a few feet away, where she'd been observing my emotional display through half-closed eyes, was Peggy Sue, my petite tabby cat. Slowly, she uncurled herself, stood up and indulged in a luxurious stretch. Then she ambled toward me in her own peculiar pigeon-toed fashion.

"Meow?" she asked, staring up at me through those sleepy green eyes. Without waiting for a reply, she gracefully maneuvered herself onto my lap. Then she wound her fluid form into a compact huddle and began to purr.

She didn't analyze me. She made no attempt to extract painful confessions or confer cliché advice. She didn't try to cheer me up. She simply made herself available.

Her pink tongue licked away the tears as they fell on her silky stripes, and Peggy Sue shared—and divided—my grief.

The Privilege of Belonging

The 15-year-old who once lived across the street called me "The Cat Lady." She knew, as did felines of every age, color, disposition and gender, that my home was a refuge for them. It was a place of security, warmth and protection from predators, abusive humans and automobiles—a place where love and Meow Mix® were freely given. Consequently, there were, at one time, three humans in our household...and twice that many cats.

Five of my furry friends "belonged" to me. Ours was a happy co-dependency. I performed the obligatory feeding, stroking, doting, admiring, loving, cat-box cleaning and healthcare arrangements. They reciprocated by preening, acting superior, and (when they deemed me worthy) settling into my lap for a catnap.

The two grey tabby homebodies, Peggy Sue and F-14 Tomcat (affectionately known as Thomas), were named for an old song and a military aircraft, respectively. Charlotte was a silver-point Siamese who pawed the doorknob and yowled "o-w-w-w-w-t" at the proper moment. (Her nickname was Genius.) She and Sarah, a coal-colored spitfire, got their names simply because I liked the sound of them. Taffy, a hot-tempered orange tabby with piercing amber eyes was named by my son during a period of his life when he was required to abstain from sugar for health reasons.

The only cat I did not consider wholly "mine" was the wild black-and-white tomcat with crossed eyes that had chosen the crawlspace beneath our mobile home as his permanent residence. Like the others, he expected his meals to be both prompt and tasty, but he would spit at my outstretched hand as I offered him sustenance.

He wouldn't allow me to hold him, caress him or enjoy the pleasant rumblings of his contented purring. He wanted only provision, not a relationship. Fear born of ignorance prevented him from trusting me, even though I wanted only to offer him the best. He remained nameless and independent.

One evening, while serving his daily meal, I noticed one of his paws was bloody and grotesquely swollen. It was apparent he had torn it open somehow—perhaps on a barbed fence or an improperly stored board with protruding nails.

I cooed and called to him in my most compelling come-hither-kitty tones, but he refused to allow my touch. Even as he limped painfully on the festering wound, he hissed a warning for me to maintain a proper distance. I would have cared for him and eased his pain, but he made it clear that he had come, as usual, for dinner—nothing more.

As I fretted in vain over his condition, I was impressed by the similarities between me and this cat who didn't belong. Before I walked with God, the wild spirit in me foolishly rejected the best, settling for an independent, but oh-so-lonely existence.

Though intellectually superior to my wild friend, I was no less ignorant of the contentment and comfort I was missing.

I did not belong to God, yet He continued to provide my daily bread—my very breath. His Word made it clear His will was that our relationship involve more commitment than merely "Provider" and "consumer." He would have alleviated my hurting and given me joy, but worldly sin remained my master.

Finally, God's wooing became irresistible. I recognized my rebellion for what it was and fell to my knees in brokenhearted repentance. God began to heal my soul of the injuries acquired by living in an ever-decaying state of sinfulness. God gave me a new heart, a new mind. My name was included in the Lamb's Book of Life. At last, I *belonged* to Him.

Now I know the benefits of being God's child. I no longer fear the unknown, for I know His protection. I enjoy His companionship and unconditional love. He's more than my Provider. He's my Friend, my Comforter, my Lord.

There came a time when we began feeling cramped in our small home, so we talked to the Savior about the possibility of His providing something a bit more spacious. He did just that, and our beloved cats Charlotte, Sarah, Thomas, Peggy Sue and Taffy all moved with us, for we were all members of one family.

I loved that standoffish little stray dearly, and I longed to be able to take him with us, too. But he belonged to our house—not to us. My heart ached when I had to leave him behind, just as I know God must grieve over the soul that rejects Him—the one who loves the world and not its Creator, the one who will be left to judgment when He comes for His own.

Just as God waited for me to repent, I anticipated the time when the feral feline would let me love him in the personal way I loved my other cats. And our Lord still patiently calls the wild ones to the foot of the cross where they will find love, forgiveness and divine fellowship.

He stands at the door, bidding sinners to open, invite Him into their hearts and trust Him completely so they may know the peace, promises and *privilege* of belonging.

Branches

In the yard in our previous residence stood a large, old willow tree, for whose summer shade we were ever grateful. However, one limb began to grow in a different direction from the rest of the tree. Instead of reaching for the heavens, it split off sideways, growing parallel to the ground. Several people bumped their heads on its lowest point. At its highest, the troublesome limb rested on our rain gutter, bending it out of shape.

So determined was the branch to "go its own way" that it became quite a nuisance. My husband was forced to remove it. In the tree's gaping wound, he carved a paraphrase of John 15:5 "I am the vine, ye are the branches...without me ye can do nothing."

A few feet away lay a pile of firewood—a reminder of the fate of the unfruitful branch.

Regrets

We shared so many hours,
good and bad.
I gave you pieces of my days,
yet never mentioned eternity.
What excuse can I give now
for allowing you to slip
from this life
while words of hope
remained chained by my tongue?
Caring I professed can now
be called a lie,
for I did not love enough
to offer you Him.

Gift

When my friend Kathleen said she had something for me, I had no reason to expect that it would be some*one.*

"She's yours," said Kathleen, beaming as she handed me a tiny tortoise shell kitten.

"I can't," I protested.

"You have to," she said.

"But I have to ask Andrew first," I stammered.

"You know your husband. He'll say yes," Kathleen countered, "Besides, she's a stray. If you don't take her, she'll have to go to the shelter. She needs you." I muttered something about taking unfair advantage of animal lovers as Kathleen continued to smile.

Looking down at the helpless creature clinging to my blouse, I cautioned my heart to be careful. Just two weeks earlier, Sarah, my feline friend of eight years, had died in my arms.

The kitten blinked her milky-blue eyes at me and cried plaintively. My wound was fresh. It was too soon to love again, I reasoned. The creature in my arms mewed again.

I heard a voice say, "I'll take her." A second later, I realized the voice was my own.

Several days had passed when Kathleen phoned to see how the kitten and I were getting along.

"She's adorable!" I crooned into the phone, "I named her Dollie."

I could tell Kathleen thought it was a silly name from the laughter in her voice when she asked why.

"Because it means 'God's gift.' I believe God gave Dollie to me because I lost Sarah."

Dollie toddled around the house during our first week together, acquainting herself with every cranny and corner. She ate well and faithfully used her litter box. By the end of the week, however, she developed diarrhea and lost her appetite.

Waiting for the doctor to see us, I relived my last visit to the clinic. I saw again Sarah's sleepy eyes and felt her velvety black body go limp as she took her final breath. Only God and I knew how much it still hurt.

Dr. Hoover examined Dollie thoroughly and tested her for some of the more common feline diseases. Her diagnosis was 'diarrhea from unknown causes.' She told me to watch Dollie carefully and feed her a special diet. I gladly agreed.

"I think you should know," began Dr. Hoover, "she's borderline." I swallowed hard, trying not to let my face register the fear welling up inside me. "She could go either way, Kim. She's small, young and fragile; she could succumb easily."

Tears clouded my vision as I drove home. *I can't lose her, Lord*, I prayed. But I did. Exactly two weeks after I'd first held her, Dollie passed away.

Two days prior to her death, Dollie refused all food and water. When I sensed the temperature of her small body beginning to drop, I wrapped her in a blanket, carrying her with me wherever I went. Having grown too weak to make her own way to the litter box, she mewed at me to take her there.

Maybe it was hope; maybe it was just denial. But until the morning Dollie died, I believed she would pull through. Later that day, Andrew helped me bury her in the corner of the rose garden. Then he held me while I sobbed into his shoulder.

I found it difficult to accept that I was burying another friend. My Creator knows how deeply I love animals. Why would God take Dollie? Her death seemed so cruel and only intensified my grief over losing Sarah. The situation seemed pretty unfair, viewing it, as I was, from the *why me* standpoint. I couldn't make sense of it and I couldn't stop grieving.

A few Saturdays later, Kathleen and I walked in the yard, absorbing the warmth of the spring sunshine. When we neared the garden, I stopped and pointed to Dollie's gravesite. Kathleen looked for a long moment at the clay-colored brick marking the kitten's final resting place.

"I'm so sorry for you," she said, turning to look into my tear-filled eyes, "but I'm glad for Dollie."

"Why do you say that?" I asked.

"Because she was a sick, suffering orphan, and I don't know anyone else who would have cared for her the way you did."

The Lord is teaching me lessons throughout this journey that He and I are on together. In my friend's words, I heard God's gentle answer to the petitions of those previous painful weeks. I'd begged Him to help me understand why Dollie had entered the void created by Sarah's death, only to be snatched away herself.

I still sometimes ache to fondle Dollie's mottled coat, just as I miss all the others who've sat in my lap purring, chasing a ribbon around the room or curled a delicate paw around my finger. Yet, the pain of these losses is eased a bit when viewed from fresh perspective.

The lesson I learned from Dollie's death has helped me deal with my human relationships, too. Now I know: in some situations, God doesn't intend for me to *receive* a gift, but simply to *be* one.

Perspective

"I've been hurt!" I say, and begin to
complain.
    "I've been lied to—betrayed!
    I deserve better..."
Then I think of One whose crown of thorns
    was placed by those
       He came to save—
and His loving plea,
    "Father, forgive them..."
The remembrance allows me
      to view my own pain—
    and self-worth—
      with proper perspective...

Blessed Detour

It was many years ago, but I still recall the details of that frosty evening. After a long wait in the grocery store check-out line, I stopped at the service desk to purchase a newspaper before heading home. Ahead of me was an elderly woman whose car had succumbed to the minus zero degree temperatures. I overheard her explaining to the clerk that she needed to use the telephone to call her husband, who was, apparently, the only person who could reason with the stubborn vehicle when it behaved this way.

When she began to place her call, I was comfortable with the knowledge that she would not be stranded. I bought my newspaper and proceeded to my car.

As I maneuvered bulky grocery bags into my trunk, I puffed out breaths that hung like clouds in the frigid night air—and uneasy thoughts of the woman with the uncooperative auto also lingered in my mind. The scene I'd just witnessed made unjustifiable my desire to check on her "just once more," but I could not squelch it.

I went back inside and found her standing at the counter where I'd left her. With desperation in her voice, she was saying, "My husband must be in the garage where he can't hear the phone ringing. I don't know *what* to do now."

"Could I take you home?" I asked, stepping up next to her. I'm usually wary of strangers, so my boldness surprised me as much as it did her, but she gratefully accepted the offer.

I dropped the woman at her home and drove another block before my own car died, refusing to be revived.

I went out of my way to help someone in need, I whined to God about the seeming unfairness of my predicament. *Why am I being "rewarded" with trouble?* Of course, the assumption that I deserved a prize for doing a good deed was more egotistical than Biblical, but crises sometimes distort my view of veracity.

I managed to coast my vehicle into a well-lit corner lot and called my husband from a pay phone. (Not everyone had cell phones in those days.) While I sat in the car awaiting his arrival, I had time to survey my surroundings more carefully. I was in a heavily populated business district with a telephone just a few yards away. The paved lot provided a safe, convenient place to park—and later to work on the car.

I realized if I'd avoided the detour required to be a blessing to another, traveling the same distance by my usual route home, I would have been stranded on a dark, winding road with few turn-outs and no telephones.

Suddenly, I was awed into a more grateful mood. And I realize now that the ability to give thanks in all circumstances[1] is sometimes acquired by simply taking a second look at what initially appears to be a problem.

---

[1] 1 Thessalonians 5:18

Spirit of "X-Mas"

"Praise to his name!" rings through the
night—
    this all-seeing one of the ages.
We read of his wisdom, goodness, and love,
    from yellowing, well-worn pages.

He gives freely, asking naught in return;
    we rejoice over what he has sent.
The spirit of modern "X-mas"—St. Nick!
    (Well, who did you think I meant?)

Your House

Choir's joyful noise and
stained-glass-filtered sunlight,
organ's intonation,
words of hope flowing from
    eloquent lips
did not this day
my spirit inspire.
Then my brother smiled
and I beheld the sweetness
    of Your visage.
I perceived Your grace
in my brother's extended hand.
Our hearts intertwined;
I tasted Christlike love.

And I was glad I had come
to Your house.

Dedicated to Jim Thacher

Too Late

When you look into his face,
his eyes reflect the pain,
that comes from serving self,
a lifetime spent in vain.

He thinks of those he called his friends,
the ones he feared would laugh,
if he chose to follow Jesus,
and take the Heavenward path.

He wonders where they've gone to—
all those valued friends—
Why have they deserted him
as he faces his life's end?

He ponders the One who promised to stay,
the One he's always shut out.
And now cries his empty human soul,
"What was my life about?"

He has a cold and aching space
the Spirit could have filled,
if only he had swallowed pride,
and surrendered stubborn will.

But he's much too tired to think now.
There's dimness in the room.
He closes his eyes—turns the Son away—
and slips into eternal doom...

Absence of Balance

Soon after committing my life to the Lord Jesus Christ, I devoted myself to various jobs in the tiny Christian fellowship to which I belonged. I assumed it was God's will for me to be involved in nearly *every* church activity, be it teaching Sunday school or Vacation Bible School, cleaning pews, attending meetings and Bible studies, editing the church newsletter, typing the bulletin, taking meals to the homebound or designing a "witness" float for a local parade.

I was impressed by the size of the potential harvest, but my mistake was thinking that I would bring it in alone instead of beseeching God to provide more laborers. And to be honest, hearing my brothers and sisters in Christ praise my abilities and my devotion was an ear-tickling—and ego-tickling—experience.

When my son began attending kindergarten, I still wasn't in the habit of praying about the many demands made on my time. I just quickened my busy walk to a run.

It took several years, but eventually my inner peace drained away. I scanned the Scriptures for a way to plug the leak, but selected only passages that validated my viewpoint.

I read that Jesus taught multitudes, so I served as room mother and playground supervisor at the private Christian school my son attended.

Jesus fed more than 5,000 people. I planned, coordinated and helped dish up lunch for the school's 300 children on special occasions.

Jesus washed the disciples' feet. I maintained a spotless home and cleaned my mother's house as well.

Sure, the Savior escaped the crowds to nourish His spirit by communicating with the Father. He rested His physical body too. But every time I came across *those* examples from Jesus' life, I countered by pointing to my full calendar.

I'd explain to God that I was claiming the promise in the book of Isaiah of being able to renew my strength, to mount up with wings like eagles, to run and not be weary, to walk and not faint. I didn't, however, abide by the conditions of the verse, which explains that this enablement is granted to those who "wait upon the Lord." (Isaiah 40:31) *I* didn't have *time* to wait!

Commotion crowded out prayer and Scripture study. My spirit continued to droop as I served others at the cost of my own spiritual growth—and health. Even when I got sick, I kept going. I couldn't—or wouldn't—stop running. Eventually I found myself feeling so ill that I couldn't rush anymore. Doctors diagnosed me with the debilitating disease Systemic Lupus Erythematosus.

Incapacitated, discouraged and in bed much of the time, I fretted over who would do the work in my place. I kept asking God why He wasn't making me better so I could get back to performing.

My frustration mounted when I was unable to meet the needs of others as I had done in the past. "I'm sorry," I would say, and then add apologetically, "All I can do is pray about it."—as if I was offering prayer as a consolation prize of some sort, instead of the powerful tool that it is.

But I did pray. I started keeping a prayer journal so that I wouldn't forget anything or anyone for whom I had made a commitment to pray. I recorded the date that I started praying, and the date of God's answers, be they "yes" or "no." Not all petitions were answered immediately, but—to my wonder and delight—many were. Others were relegated to the "wait" category.

As I sat propped in bed, I began to spend more time reading Scripture, too. My Bible studies became times of sweet fellowship with God as He spoke to me through His Word. I started to realize that I had allowed pandemonium to drown out His quiet voice of wisdom and love. I covenanted to continue daily Bible study whether I was sick or well.

Even though my ailment is currently considered incurable, I soon became able to get out of bed more often, so I was able to maintain my home (settling for less than perfect order), nurture my family and continue my prayer ministry.

A .W. Tozer wrote, "The simplicity which is in Christ is rarely found among us. In its stead are programs, methods, organizations and a world of nervous activities that occupy time and attention but can never satisfy the longing of the heart. We, in this day, know God imperfectly, and the peace of God scarcely at all."[2]

Peer pressure can make it difficult for a people-pleaser with even the best intentions to say "no." However, experience has taught me that that "yes" is not always the godly response. In some situations, "yes" may be a satanic trap that siphons energy, making us ineffective for Christ.

Absence of balance paved the way to my burnout—and just as proper medication and proper care are necessary to control my disease—Bible study and quiet times with the Lord Jesus are essential to my spiritual health. If I don't *keep* that balance in my life,

---

[2] *The Pursuit of God*, by A. W. Tozer, ©1948 Christian Publications, Inc., Harrisburg, PA

my busyness and service can easily become disobedience. Then clutter again replaces worship and clatter once more drowns out the voice of God.

Grandma Gave Me Heaven

More than merely my "mother's mother," Grandma Vivian and I had a special connection. It seemed no one understood me like she did. She was my first confidant and friend.

This lady with the laughing eyes generously gave me her time and affection (as well as Play-doh®, dolls, stuffed animals, candy...) in my early years. Her acceptance and understanding instilled me with a sense of security and belonging.

When I was five years old, our family made a move that put 2,000 miles between Grandma and me. I was devastated, but she helped me adjust to the loss by teaching me to write letters. She sent me packages of self-addressed, stamped envelopes to make it easy. Mama invited Grandma to our new home in Utah for yearly visits. When I grew older, it was I who annually flew cross-country.

During one of our summer reunions at Grandma's home in North Carolina, I turned fourteen. That was the year Grandma bestowed upon me the most precious gift of all.

It was a characteristically muggy day when Grandma and I went to the Christian bookstore near her home. The smell of old, creaking wood floors pervaded my senses. I remember the excitement in Grandma's face when she stooped to look directly into mine.

"Will you promise to read this if I buy it?" asked Grandma, beaming. I nodded enthusiastically and accepted the Bible she offered. At the time, I was a member, though inactive, of an organization that ridiculed the Bible as inferior to man's teachings and proclaimed it unreliable. I was, consequently acquainted with the teachings of my religion's founder and "prophet," but largely unfamiliar with the Holy Scriptures.

I was so curious about the contents of my new mysterious book that I spent the rest of my visit plying Grandma with questions—sometimes until morning's wee hours. She taught me to utilize the Bible's reference features to find desired information.

When our time together ended, I went back to Utah, where the adolescent years found me asking new questions: *Why am I here? Who loves me? Why do I feel empty inside?* I forgot my vow to Grandma that I would search the Scriptures when I needed help.

My Bible gathered dust as I sought solutions to life's riddles in a study of astrology and the occult. Discontent grew like a fungus within me and I sought to thwart it with alcohol consumption.

The sin of drunkenness only compounded my problems. Four years after accepting my grandmother's gift, I was a suicidal teen struggling to deal with the physical and emotional ramifications of an abortion.

I blamed God—whoever He was—for my troubles. I was unwilling to accept my misery and guilt as natural consequences of my own choices.

At age nineteen I married Andrew, an incredible, caring man. Our son, Leon was born eighteen months later. I reveled in our strong love for one another. Yet, the hollow place in my heart remained void. In desperation, I cried out to a God I hardly knew, pleading with Him to save me from this emptiness I felt.

He responded by invoking memories of Grandma's gift from years earlier. Suddenly, I found myself drawn to the Bible—and to North Carolina.

Eager to please me, my husband, Andrew, agreed to leave his home state and move to mine. We sold nearly all of our personal possessions to get enough money for the relocation. Then the four of us—Andrew, Leon, me and my Bible—boarded a bus to make the three-day journey across the country.

There, Andrew and I found work on a dairy farm. Leon seemed to thrive in the sweet country air. Our intelligent bovine "co-workers" gave us much pleasure, and the hard work gave us ravenous appetites.

Even more voracious, though, was my appetite for God's Word. In its pages, I found answers long sought. I discovered my emptiness was a by-product of alienation from God caused by my sin nature. I learned that God was not the angry killjoy propagated by some, but a loving, merciful Being who desired a relationship with *me*.

One evening, after Andrew and Leon had gone to sleep, I sat alone in the small ramshackle house that constituted a portion of our salary.

I listened to crickets' melodious chirping and the gentle jangling of the herd's neck chains as they milled about outside my open window. And I listened to the voice of God as He spoke to me from the pages of the Bible spread across my lap.

A shocking, but undeniable truth pierced my consciousness. *My human sinfulness would always prevent me from being "good enough" to get to Heaven. Without Christ, I was doomed to Hell!*

The next moment, I was begging my Creator for forgiveness. "I want my life to be Yours," I told Him. Immediately, He infused me with His Spirit—His guarantee that I belonged securely to Him. For the first time in my life, my heart was at peace.

Shortly after that, our living situation deteriorated rapidly as Satan threw a temper tantrum over losing one of his followers. Our employer began to engage in unethical business practices, along with sexually harassing me. Andrew and I were forced to resign our positions. For the second time in less than one year, we were unemployed and homeless. Yet, even as we drifted from cheap motels to KOA campgrounds, I felt *no fear*.

By the time the snow began to fall in the Rockies, Andrew, Leon and I were safely back in Utah, taken there by God's faithfulness.

Many years have passed since I accepted the Lord Jesus Christ as my Savior and surrendered my whole heart and soul to Him. I've renounced my membership in that organization that criticizes the Bible. Andrew and Leon are both Believers as well, and all of us have received Christian baptism. Andrew and I renewed our wedding vows in a Christian church, since we'd left God out of our first ceremony. I continued to write to or telephone Grandma nearly every week until Alzheimer's made her forget who I was. She went to be with the Lord sixteen years ago, and I inherited *her* Bible.

Its once-shiny black cover has fallen off, the pages discolored and separating from the binding. But its truths are eternally resilient. They have set me free, just as Christ promised in John 8:32.

The power of God's Word liberated me from sin's control. It gave me the capacity to know and love God, to nurture my marriage, to raise our son with godly principles, to live with purpose and faith.

Inside the front cover of the tattered book Grandma gave me—the book whose words saved my soul and enrich my life daily—is this inscription: *"Presented to Kim on this day, given in love and devotion to you...Always put Christ first and you will never go wrong...Granny."*

Grandma's many varied gifts never failed to give me pleasure. But when she gave me the Word that was with God—and *is God*—Grandma gave me Heaven.

"Thomas and the Doubter" was originally published in *Power For Living*

"Wedding Prayer" was originally published in *Quilt World*

"The Storm" was originally published in *Decision Magazine*

"Flowers for my Birthday" was originally published in *The Salt Lake Tribune*

"Like Father" was originally published in *Bible Advocate*

"Dragon Mommy" was originally published in *For Parents*

"Holiday Religion" was originally published in *The Rescue Mission of Salt Lake Newsletter*

"Before your Throne" was originally published in *Decision Magazine*

"Your Voice" was originally published in *Decision Magazine*

"Sunday Morning" was originally published in *Woman's Touch*

"New Heart's Resolutions" was originally published in *Decision Magazine*

"Living with Killing" was originally published in *Seek*

"Divine Docket" was originally published in *Decision Magazine*

"The Privilege of Belonging" was originally published in *Power For Living*

Kimberly Malkogainnis

"Branches" was originally published in *Inspirer Magazine*

"Regrets" was originally published in *Decision Magazine*

"Perspective" was originally published in *Decision Magazine*

"Blessed Detour" was originally published in *Evangel Magazine*

"Spirit of "X-Mas"" was originally published in *Pocket Inspirations*

"Your House" was originally Published in *Decision Magazine*

"Absence of Balance" was originally published in *Decision Magazine*

"Grandma Gave Me Heaven" was originally published in *The Message of the Open Bible*

About the Author

Kimberly Malkogainnis resides in the quiet, historic mining town of Copperton, Utah, population 1000, with her beloved husband of 36 years. She is blessed to have her son, his wife and her four grandchildren as next-door neighbors. Kimberly has been writing nearly all her life, but began writing for God's glory about 25 years ago. Her favorite Bible verse is I John 4:10: *"Here is love: not that we loved God, but that He loved us and sent His Son to be the atoning sacrifice for our sins."*

If you'd like to contact the author, you may send her an email at kimmalkos@hotmail.com or write to her in care of Next Step Books, P.O. Box 70271, West Valley City, UT 84170.

9 781937 671105